D1307038

WOODCHUCKS

Amy-Jane Beer

Grolier
an imprint of

SCHOLASTIC

www.scholastic.com/librarypublishing

Published 2008 by Grolier
An imprint of Scholastic Library Publishing
Old Sherman Turnpike, Danbury,
Connecticut 06816

For The Brown Reference Group plc
Project Editor: Jolyon Goddard
Copy-editors: Lesley Ellis, Lisa Hughes,
    Wendy Horobin
Picture Researcher: Clare Newman
Designers: Jeni Child, Lynne Ross,
    Sarah Williams
Managing Editor: Bridget Giles

Volume ISBN-13: 978-0-7172-6267-0
Volume ISBN-10: 0-7172-6267-7

**Library of Congress
Cataloging-in-Publication Data**

Nature's children. Set 2.
    p. cm.
    Includes bibliographical references and
index.
    ISBN-13: 978-0-7172-8081-0
    ISBN-10: 0-7172-8081-0
    1. Animals--Encyclopedias, Juvenile. 1.
Grolier (Firm)
    QL49.N383 2007
    590--dc22
                        2007026928

Printed and bound in China

PICTURE CREDITS

Front Cover: **Shutterstock**: Hway Kiong
Lim

Back Cover: **Nature PL**: Lynn M. Stone;
NHPA: Stephen Krasemann; **Shutterstock**:
Bruce MacQueen

Alamy: FS Agency 4, 17, Imagebroker 38;
Corbis: Gary W. Carter 21, Christof
Wermter/zefa 45; **Natural Visions**: Heather
Angel 37; **NHPA**: Stephen Krasemann 5, 29,
30; **Photolibrary.com**: Gordon and Cathy
Illg 42, Zigmund Leszczynski 34;
Photos.com: 26–27, 33, 46; **Shutterstock**:
Kevin Chesson 41, Chrita De Ridder 10, Alan
Gleichman 14, Hway Kiong Lim 2–3, 6, Bruce
MacQueen 18, 22, Rickt 9; **Still Pictures**: H.
Schulze 13.

Contents

FACT FILE: Woodchucks

Class	Mammals (Mammalia)
Order	Rodents (Rodentia)
Family	Squirrels (Sciuridae)
Genus	Marmots (*Marmota*)
Species	Woodchuck (*Marmota monax*)
World distribution	North America
Habitat	Mixed woods, open forests, and pastures
Distinctive physical characteristics	Stout body, with short, thick neck and tail, and pointed face; fur is shaggy and grizzled brown
Habits	Lives alone or in pairs in an underground burrow; active by day, from April to November; hibernates in winter
Diet	Fresh green leaves and shoots, fruit, roots, twigs, and bark

Introduction

Woodchucks are a type of ground squirrel. Ground squirrels don't climb trees. They find food on the ground and shelter in underground **burrows**. Unlike other ground squirrels, such as marmots, which live in groups, woodchucks prefer to live alone. Woodchucks are rodents, like mice, beavers, and cavies. All rodents have constantly growing front teeth that they use for gnawing. After a busy spring, summer, and fall, woodchucks are ready to rest. They spend winter in a deep sleep called **hibernation**.

A young woodchuck sits outside its burrow.

A woodchuck,
or groundhog, looks
for some food.

6

What's Its Name?

Woodchucks are known by all sorts of different names. The name woodchuck comes from the Native American word *otcheck*—which was actually what the Native Americans called the fisher, a relative of weasels. Early European settlers who traded furs with Native Americans thought the name referred to the animal now known as the woodchuck. The settlers also continually mispronounced *otcheck*, and so the word got turned into "woodchuck."

Woodchucks are often called **groundhogs**. It's not hard to see why. These chubby animals eat a lot and live underground. Some people call woodchucks **whistle pigs**—for the loud whistles they make when they are alarmed.

Woodchucks are often confused with a similar-looking animal called a **marmot**. Marmots live in Europe, Asia, and North America. Marmots and woodchucks are so closely related that they could breed together if they lived in the same regions.

One Fat Squirrel!

Woodchucks are members of the squirrel family. They don't look much like squirrels, do they? They don't have a long, bushy tail and they can't climb trees. That is because they are ground squirrels, not tree squirrels. Tree squirrels use their tail to stay balanced on the high branches, much like a tightrope walker uses a pole. But woodchucks usually stay on the ground. With four feet firmly on the ground, balance is not a problem—and a long tail would simply get in the way.

One of the woodchuck's other close relatives is the prairie dog—and there the family resemblance is a little more obvious. Prairie dogs are ground squirrels, too.

A prairie dog sits on its hind legs as it checks out its surroundings.

The yellow-bellied marmot is a close relative of the woodchuck.

Marmots of America

There are six species, or types, of marmots that live in America. The woodchuck is one of these species. Woodchucks are better known than most other marmot species. That is because woodchucks live in places where they are more likely to be seen by people, such as grasslands and prairie edges. Most other marmot species are small, hardy mountain animals.

The Olympic marmot lives in Washington State, while the yellow-bellied marmot lives in the Rocky Mountains of Canada and the United States. The hoary marmot ranges from Alaska through western Canada to the northwestern United States. The Alaska marmot lives in, you've guessed it, Alaska! The rarest marmot is the Vancouver Island marmot. There are only a few hundred Vancouver Island marmots still alive. Many of them live in zoos.

Cousins Overseas

There are marmots in Asia and Europe, too. The woodchuck's largest close relative is called the **alpine** marmot. It lives in the mountains of southern Europe, where the winters are very long and cold. Alpine marmots can weigh up to 10 pounds (4.5 kg). The extra fat helps keep them warm.

The main difference between woodchucks and many of their cousins is that, unlike woodchucks, most other marmots live in large family groups. Compared to young woodchucks, who might be on their own from six weeks old, the young of mountain-dwelling marmots live with their parents for two or three years before heading out on their own. The harsh alpine winters make it too difficult for young marmots to survive alone, so they stay together—huddled and warm in their burrows.

Alpine marmots have a lot of body fat, which helps keep them warm.

13

By balancing on its back legs, a woodchuck can get a better view.

Living Dangerously

Living on the ground can be dangerous for animals the size of woodchucks. They are too big to hide among the grass from the sharp eyes of **predators**. Woodchucks have many enemies including eagles, foxes, coyotes, and bobcats.

To remain safe, woodchucks need to be extremely alert. They have a great sense of smell and very sensitive ears. As well as listening for sounds of predators, woodchucks also listen for alarm whistles from other woodchucks. Every so often, they rear onto their back legs to get a good look around. With all of those sharp senses tuned in to detect danger, woodchucks can usually get to a safe place before a predator has a chance to attack.

Ready, Get Set, Dig!

Woodchucks are built for digging. Their thickset body makes them look a little overweight, but they have the perfect shape for digging—short, strong legs and big muscles in their shoulders and back. Many other great diggers, such as badgers, wombats, and moles, have a similar body shape. The woodchuck also has strong claws for loosening hard-packed soil. Its large front teeth are used to cut away roots that get in the way. It can even use its flat-topped head like a bulldozer shovel to push stones and soil around!

Woodchucks use their large, strong claws to hold food and dig burrows.

17

A woodchuck peers out from the entrance to its burrow.

Burrow Below

A woodchuck's underground home is called a
burrow. In summer, woodchucks live in burrows
they've dug from well-drained soil, close to a
good supply of food. The simplest burrows have
a short tunnel with a small sleeping chamber
at the end. But as time goes by, the burrow's
owner digs more tunnels, more rooms, and
more entrances. Some older woodchucks
have burrows that run 50 feet (15 m) or
more underground, with four or five different
entrances. Often, one of these entrances is the
emergency **plunge hole**. The woodchuck will
disappear into this vertical shaft if it is being
chased by predators.

Household Chores

Woodchucks are very clean animals. They spend a lot of time tidying up their burrow. Inside the burrow is a separate room, which the woodchuck uses when it needs to relieve itself. The rest of the tunnels and other burrow rooms stay quite clean. The woodchuck uses its large flat feet to sweep loose soil and other dirt out of the tunnels. There is normally a pile of dirt outside the main entrance to a woodchuck's burrow.

The woodchuck's bedroom is usually stuffed with leaves and dry grass to make a comfortable sleeping area. The woodchuck also changes the bedding regularly. It throws out the old grass and leaves when they get damp or stale and then goes in search of some fresh new material.

A woodchuck carries some grass and twigs to its burrow.

21

A woodchuck marks the edge of its territory.

Private, Keep Out

Adult woodchucks usually live alone and do not welcome company. They like to keep their burrow and **territory** private. But instead of putting up fences and "keep out" signs they use smelly markers to stop other woodchucks from coming in.

Woodchucks have a **gland** near their tail that leaks small amounts of personal scent every time the woodchuck relieves itself. Every day, as the woodchuck goes about its business, it leaves little heaps of droppings and splashes of urine around its territory. These markers tell other woodchucks exactly which animal lives in the area. The droppings also tell them to stay away.

Personal Space

The size of a female woodchuck's territory depends on how much food is available. Although female woodchucks are smaller than males, in summer they have to eat more food. They need a lot of nutrients in order to produce milk to feed their young. Determining how much land they need is a bit tricky. The territory must be large enough to provide the right amount of food. But it can't be too big, or the female will have to waste energy defending it. Usually, a female woodchuck's territory is around the size of one or two soccer fields.

Male woodchucks don't have to feed their young, so it would seem logical that they would have a smaller territory. Actually, they have a much larger territory than a female's—up to the size of seven soccer fields. Having a bigger territory means that a male has more female neighbors. When spring comes along, every male wants to **mate** with as many females as he can.

So Much to Do

Spring is the busiest season for woodchucks. In March or April, they move from their winter **den** in the woods back out to the open pastures. After a long winter with little food available, they are starving and spend many hours a day simply eating. But there is other work to be done, too. Each woodchuck might have to fight to claim back its summer territory. Then it has to give the burrow a good spring cleaning, repair damaged tunnels, clear blockages, and collect fresh bedding.

If that wasn't enough, there is also something else the woodchuck has to do—something very important. Spring is the woodchuck's breeding season. Adult woodchucks have to start thinking about having a family right away. They have only around six months in which to raise their young before winter comes again. If they don't breed immediately, the babies will still be too small by fall to survive the winter.

A woodchuck eats some clover in a field full of flowers.

26

A New Family

Baby woodchucks are born around a month after the male and female woodchucks mate. There are usually four or five babies in each **litter**. They are born on a bed of grass, which keeps them warm. The mother has to change the bedding regularly. The babies take a few weeks to learn to use the area designated for relieving themselves. They need a few weeks to learn how to keep themselves clean.

Each newborn woodchuck weighs around 1 ounce (30 g). These tiny, pink babies are covered in thin, downy fur, their eyes are closed, and they can only crawl on their legs.

For the first few weeks, baby woodchucks depend entirely on their mother. She visits them several times a day to feed them milk. When she leaves, they huddle together for warmth until their fur coat thickens and they put on weight.

After around four weeks, the youngsters begin to go outside the burrow. They stay close to the entrance at first, but soon gain confidence and begin exploring the surrounding area.

A young woodchuck stays close to the entrance of its burrow.

A woodchuck mother looks after one of her babies.

Facing Life Alone

Woodchuck mothers look after their young for around six weeks. By then, the babies are fully weaned—they can eat adult food and no longer need milk. However, there is not enough food in the mother woodchuck's territory to go around. In her own way, she lets the young woodchucks know that it is time to leave. Sometimes if the territory has a lot of spare food, she allows one or two of her daughters to stay. They will then all share the territory. But most young woodchucks must travel some distance to find an area with plenty of food and no other woodchucks. They often find an old abandoned den and make that their new home.

Fresh Greens

A woodchuck likes nothing better than a field of fresh greens. Their favorite summer foods are plants, such as alfalfa, clover, and buttercups. In late summer and fall, when plants have ripe seeds, woodchucks eat many of these, too. Seeds contain a lot of protein and fat, which help woodchucks put on weight before winter.

Sometimes woodchucks are tempted to nibble crops, such as corn, cabbages, and beets. Not surprisingly, farmers don't like that. So, they try to fence out the woodchucks. The trouble is, woodchucks are such good diggers that they can burrow under the fences in no time. A woodchuck-proof fence has to go down into the ground as well as up into the air!

Woodchucks like to eat buttercups and clover.

A woodchuck enjoys eating some maize.

Living Together

Hundreds of years ago, when European pioneers began to settle in America, they made many changes to the landscape. They cleared several of the forests for firewood and to make pastures for their cattle. They also worked very hard to make areas of wilderness suitable for planting crops. That meant clearing rocks and boulders, digging **drainage** ditches, and plowing and tilling the land. They then sowed seeds and spent the summers carefully weeding and tending their crops. Imagine, after all that work, how upset they must have been when they discovered that small, furry animals were getting fat by stealing crops from their fields!

The farmers didn't realize it at first, but the changes they had made to the land made it perfect for woodchucks. Removing the stones and draining away the water made the soil much easier for woodchucks to dig. With a ready supply of fresh food planted nearby, the woodchucks moved in!

Too Many?

Stealing food isn't the only thing woodchucks do to upset people. Often, their busy burrowing can cause problems. Their digging can cause fence posts to loosen and fall down. Horses often catch their feet in woodchuck holes, causing them to stumble and possibly injure themselves and their rider. In many places, woodchucks are hunted to keep their numbers under control. Some people eat them, too!

Woodchucks aren't always bad news, however. They also do some good. Like all wild creatures, they play an important part in nature. For example, their burrows help mix air into the soil, which makes the soil more suitable for growing plants and crops. The animals are also a source of food for many other types of wildlife.

The holes woodchucks dig in fields and parks make the animals a nuisance to many people.

The alpine marmot has large front teeth, sharp enough to fight off a predator.

Brave Fighter

Sometimes, through bad luck or the speed and skill of a predator, woodchucks find themselves trapped and unable to escape into the safety of their burrow. But woodchucks are very brave animals and they never give up without a fight. After all, they're not completely defenseless—they have strong claws and extremely sharp teeth.

When cornered, a woodchuck turns around to face its attacker. It does its best to look as large and fierce as possible. It fluffs up its fur and opens its mouth to show off its big front teeth. It also makes a growling noise and grinds its teeth together angrily. If the predator comes close enough, the woodchuck springs up and sinks its teeth into whatever flesh it can reach. That is often enough of a shock to make the predator jump away, which gives the woodchuck one last chance to make a run to safety.

Sleeping in the Sun

Woodchucks love to sunbathe. Early in the morning, they are often a little chilled after sleeping in a cool, damp burrow. Aboveground, they usually have a favorite spot to sit, stretch out, and soak up the warm sunshine.

The Sun is nature's clock and calendar. The position of the Sun in the sky, and the length of time it appears in the sky each day, help animals know what time of day and which season it is. The Sun triggers changes in each woodchuck's body. These changes ensure they are ready to breed at the same time, that they grow a thin summer coat in spring, and that they start putting on weight in fall.

A woodchuck lies on a log as it soaks up the sun.

In fall, a woodchuck begins to prepare for a long, winter hibernation.

42

Long Goodnight

Woodchucks know it is time for a long winter sleep when the days begin to get shorter and food becomes harder to find. In late fall, grass and other plants stop growing because they don't get enough sunlight. For the first time in months, woodchucks go hungry. The fat they have put on over summer won't last all winter if they keep waking up and moving around every day. The only way to make their body fat last is to go into a very deep sleep, called hibernation.

When the time comes to hibernate, a woodchuck blocks the entrance to its winter burrow with grass and leaves. Inside the burrow, it curls up, closes its eyes, and slowly sinks into a sleep so deep that the animal seems almost dead. The woodchuck's body temperature drops so much that it feels cold. Its heart beats only once every 10 or 15 seconds, and the woodchuck takes only about one breath every five minutes.

Winter Retreat

A woodchuck's winter den is quite different from its summer burrow. The woodchuck uses its winter den only for sleeping in, so the den doesn't need to be very big. But it does need to be safe. It is possible, under the weight of the snow, for a tunnel to collapse during winter and bury the woodchuck alive while it sleeps. A tunnel collapse is much more likely to happen in the loose sandy soils in which the summer burrow is built. Therefore, woodchucks choose to build their winter burrows in more densely packed soil, which is at less risk of collapsing.

The winter burrow is usually positioned at the base of a tree, where the roots help support it. In a forest, there is also more shelter from the wind, snow, and rain. The ground doesn't become quite as cold as it does in the open. The winter den doesn't need a large territory attached to it for feeding. The woodchuck won't be eating anything until it wakes up in the spring!

Plenty of bedding
is needed for the
winter hibernation.

Once a woodchuck has woken from its hibernation, it needs to start eating immediately.

Rise and Shine!

It takes a woodchuck several hours to wake up fully after its long winter sleep. Its body is chilled to the core, and it can barely move. The woodchuck immediately begins to shiver. That gets the woodchuck's muscles working again, and its heart starts to beat faster. The woodchuck starts breathing faster, too, taking short wheezy puffs. After a while, the woodchuck can begin to move. It stretches and scratches and then takes a few big yawns. After that, it's time for the woodchuck to unblock the entrance to its burrow and go outside. The woodchuck hasn't eaten for a long time and immediately goes in search of food.

Groundhog Day

The second day of February is Groundhog Day. Have you ever wondered how woodchucks came to have a day named for them? According to tradition, woodchucks (or groundhogs) wake up on February 2nd each year and take a look outside. Legend has it that if they can see their shadow, there will be another six weeks of winter before the spring weather arrives. So, if it's sunny on Groundhog Day, be prepared for snow! The sensible groundhog gives up and goes back to bed until March or April. But if February 2nd is an overcast day and the groundhogs can't see their shadow, it means spring is not far away. The groundhogs then stay out of their burrows and start preparing for spring.

Words to Know

Alpine From the Alps, a mountain range in Europe; sometimes means from mountainous areas in general.

Burrows Holes in the ground dug by animals to use as homes.

Den An animal's home.

Drainage The way water runs out of soil, leaving it dry and easy to dig.

Gland An organ that produces substances that help keep the body working. Milk, sweat, stomach juices, and scent all come from glands.

Groundhogs Another name for woodchucks.

Hibernation A very deep winter sleep that saves an animal's energy.

Litter	A group of baby animals born together.
Marmot	Another name for a woodchuck and related animals.
Mate	To come together to produce young.
Plunge hole	An opening directly down into a woodchuck's burrow used as an emergency escape route.
Predators	Animals that hunt and eat other animals.
Territory	The patch of land an animal or group of animals treats as private space, and guards from others of the same species.
Whistle pigs	Another name for woodchucks.

Find Out More

Books

Old, W. C. *The Groundhog Day Book of Facts and Fun*.
Moreton Grove, Illinois: Albert Whitman and
Company, 2004.

Richardson, A. D. *Groundhogs: Woodchucks, Marmots,
and Whistle Pigs*. Wild World of Animals. Minneapolis,
Minnesota: Bridgestone Books/Capstone Press, 2002.

Web sites

Animal Diversity
*animaldiversity.ummz.umich.edu/site/accounts/
information/Marmota_monax.html*
Includes information and photographs.

Enchanted Learning
*www.enchantedlearning.com/subjects/mammals/rodent/
Groundhogprintout.shtml*
Facts about woodchucks, and pictures to print and color in.

Index